PUSH AND PULL

by Robin Nelson

first step nonfiction

Lerner Publications Company · Minneapolis

A **force** can be a **push.**

A force can be a **pull.**

Pushing can **move** something.

Pulling can move something.

A push can change the way something is moving.

A pull can change the way
something is moving.

A push can start
something moving.

A push can stop
something moving.

A pull can start
something moving.

A pull can stop
something moving.

You can pull a **kite.**

You can push a swing.

You can pull a sled.

You can push a toy train.

What can you push?

What can you pull?

pulley

rope

A Pulley

Machines can make pushing and pulling easier. One machine that can help us pull is called a pulley. A pulley is a wheel with a rope around it. The wheel turns when you pull on the rope. Flagpoles have pulleys to help lift the flag. Can you find other pulleys?

Push and Pull Facts

 Gravity is a force that pulls things to the earth.

 Magnets pull some objects to them. Magnets push some objects away from them.

 Sled dog racing is a sport in Alaska and other cold parts of the world. A team of dogs pulls a driver riding on a sled over the ice and snow.

A man once pulled a big jet airplane almost 300 feet.

 A push-up is an exercise. You lie face down on the ground and push your body up with your arms.

 The most push-ups done in one hour is 3,416.

 Wings push birds into the sky.

Glossary

 force – a push or a pull

 kite – a covered frame that is attached to a piece of string and is flown in the wind

 move – to go from one place to another

 pull – to make something move toward you

 push – to make something move away from you

Index

The photographs in this book are reproduced through the courtesy of: Brand X Pictures, cover, p. 13; © Norbert Schaefer/CORBIS, pp. 2, 22 (top and bottom); Photodisc Royalty Free by Getty Images, pp. 3, 22 (second from bottom); © Anton Vengo/SuperStock, pp. 4, 22 (middle); © Bruce Burkhardt/CORBIS, p. 5; © Todd Strand/Independent Picture Service, pp. 6, 9, 15; © Diane Meyer, p. 7; Stockbyte Royalty Free, p. 8; © Lisette Le Bon/SuperStock, p. 10; Comstock Royalty-Free, p. 11; © Tim Kiusalaas/CORBIS, pp. 12, 22 (second from top); Corbis Royalty Free, p. 14; © Tom & Dee Ann McCarthy/CORBIS, p. 16; © Ariel Skelley/CORBIS, p. 17.

Illustration on page 18 by Laura Westlund.

Lerner Publications Company
A division of Lerner Publishing Group
241 First Avenue North
Minneapolis, MN 55401 USA

Website address: www.lernerbooks.com

Library of Congress Cataloging-in-Publication Data

Nelson, Robin, 1971–
    Push and pull / by Robin Nelson.
        p.   cm. — (First step nonfiction)
    Includes index.
    Summary: Simple text introduces the different effects that pushing and pulling can have on objects.
    ISBN: 0–8225–5134–9 (lib. bdg. : alk. paper)
    1. Force and energy—Juvenile literature. [1. Force and energy.] I. Title. II. Series.
QC73.4.N45 2004
531'.6—dc22   2003013888

Manufactured in the United States of America
1 2 3 4 5 6 – DP – 09 08 07 06 05 04